THE BIG GREEN POETRY MACHINE

Amazing Words

Edited By Allie Jones

First published in Great Britain in 2023 by:

 YoungWriters®
Est. 1991

Young Writers
Remus House
Coltsfoot Drive
Peterborough
PE2 9BF
Telephone: 01733 890066
Website: www.youngwriters.co.uk

Printed and bound in the UK by BookPrintingUK
Website: www.bookprintinguk.com
YB0541Y

FOREWORD

Welcome Reader,

For Young Writers' latest competition The Big Green Poetry Machine, we asked primary school pupils to craft a poem about the world. From nature and environmental issues to exploring their own habitats or those of others around the globe, it provided pupils with the opportunity to share their thoughts and feelings about the world around them.

Here at Young Writers our aim is to encourage creativity in children and to inspire a love of the written word, so it's great to get such an amazing response, with some absolutely fantastic poems. It's important for children to be aware of the world around them and some of the issues we face, but also to celebrate what makes it great! This competition allowed them to express their hopes and fears or simply write about their favourite things. The Big Green Poetry Machine gave them the power of words and the result is a wonderful collection of inspirational and moving poems in a variety of poetic styles.

I'd like to congratulate all the young poets in this anthology; I hope this inspires them to continue with their creative writing.

NATURE   WILDLIFE   INSECTS   EARTH   RECYCLE

CONTENTS

Ezmae Donegal (7) 64
Priyal Karavadra (11) 65
Maja Nicka (10) 66
Alicija Gadaj (11) 67
Eduard Atudorei (8) 68
Eva Pavlovecova (10) 69
Alfie Harte (6) 70
Archie Fox (7) 71
Esmai Wilson (11) 72
Harvey-Lee McKenzie (6) 73
Aaron Dunkely (11) 74
Savanna Britton (9) 75
Jasper Sharp (6) 76
Flourish Arifalo (11) 77
Andreea Sterea (9) 78
Artiom Adomnita (5) 79
Ryan George (11) 80
Maja Cieslik (10) 81
Ruby Wilson (6) 82
Ryley Kelly (9) 83
Penny Woods (7) 84
Oyindamola Nuga (6) 85
Darcy Millar (5) 86
Gloria Nasonkina (5) 87
Elliott York (5) 88
Maddison-Amara Culhane (6) 89
Reginald Manu (6) 90
Monica Allen (8) 91
Leighton Mickenzie (9) 92
Nyla-Rose Lewis (8) 93
Madalina Dorofei (5) 94
Niamh Mayhew (6) 95
Samuel Allen (5) 96
Dimitri Matran (8) 97
Mia Murphy (8) 98
Jaiden Clark (10) 99
Geon Gilin (6) 100
Jacob Franklin (6) 101
Saphire-Ruby Garrett (6) 102
Chelsea Konadu (9) 103
Niamh Kenny (11) 104
Ellie Burley (5) 105
Stefania Rotaru (9) 106

Zara Bittar (5) 107
Logan Rowland (6) 108

McKinney Primary School, Dundrod

James McClure (8) 109
Luxie Milliken (8) 110
Olly Jay (8) 111
Julianne Craig (7) 112
Lexi Bryans (8) 113
Chloe Watson (7) 114
Anna Nicholson (7) 115
Priscilla Bell (7) 116
Maisie Bamford (8) 117
Evie Minford (8) 118
Matthew Flanagan (7) 119
Nate Dawson (8) 120
Coleen Harbinson (8) 121
Luke Montgomery (8) 122
Harrison Brown (8) 123
Ryan Duckett (8) 124
Martha Dunlop (8) 125
Charlotte Brown (7) 126
Annie Gordon (7) 127
Flynn Allison (7) 128
Lewis Park (7) 129
Dawson Baker (8) 130

Sacred Heart RC Primary School, Blackburn

Zahra Shahbaz (8) 131
Adela Dahdouh (9) 132
Aisha Ashfaq (9) 135
Atiya Zain Iqbal (8) 136
Aiza Hussain (9) 137
Aira Kashif (8) 138
Ziya Patel (9) 139
Aleena Kamal (8) 140
Eryka Aldea (9) 141
Adam Mohamed (8) 142
Ummay Fatima Bhatti (9) 143
Amalia Nasukhanova (9) 144

Rukaia Ibrahim (9) 145

Somerset Bridge Primary School, Bridgwater

Elliott Gardner (8) 146
Kristian Wheeler (7) 147
Florence Bunce (8) 148

St Cuthbert's Catholic Primary School, Walbottle Village

Callum Naylor (10) 149
Nyle Hassan (9) 150
Ella Leddicoat (9) 151
Alfie Daymond (10) 152
Olivier Belzynski (9) 153
Hamiz Khan (10) 154
Gabriella Hewson (9) 155
Billy Doyle (10) 156
Amaan Qaiser (9) 157
Eva Costigan (9) 158
Rafay Ishaque (10) 159
John Jennings (10) 160
Aleena Ismail (10) 161
Robson Doyle (9) 162
Heidi Blackett (9) 163
Amelia Hardy (9) 164
Jess Mciver (10) 165
Edward Dodgson (9) 166
Maisie Rodelas (9) 167
Alfie Gray (10) 168
Maria Khaliq (9) 169
Zaara Zafar (10) 170
Husnain Jawed (10) 171
Francesca McRoberts (10) 172
Beau Shearer (10) 173
Max Towns (9) 174

St Joseph's Primary School, Gabalfa

Leo Makzal (7) 175
Jumaima Uddin (7) 176

Teddy Bowen (7) 177
Jacob Williams (7) 178
Aadil Maghal (8) 179
Noah Diaz (8) 180
Ire Balogun (8) 181

The Elms Junior School, Long Eaton

Nikita Neverov (7) 182
Sophia Baldwin (9) 186
Freya Baldwin (9) 187
Heather Irving (8) 188
Mareck Yarlett (9) 189
Avani Athwal (10) 190
Jack Chambers (8) 191
Ziyu (Andy) Guo (7) 192
Emily Walters (6) 193
Torben Brennan (6) 194
Thomas Borkowski (5) 195
Hermione Wilson-Gallaher (9) 196
Eve Howat (8) 197
Joe Canton (8) 198
Eden Faulkner (10) 199
Bella Sparling (10) 200
Leah Sood (8) 201
Rosie Faulkner (6) 202

THE POEMS

Trees, Oh Trees

Trees, oh trees,
Trees are home to bumblebees,
I don't like it when my branches are full of waste,
And getting chopped down is not to my taste,
I allow children to climb me to a degree,
But when I'm alone I let my branches flow free,
Just like you, I have my very own family,
But when we get chopped down we get separated
rapidly,
When I grow the whole galaxy wants to see,
But when I'm old no one really cares about me,
Think about me when you come across a tree,
I will stop you from doing bad things to my family,
Yes me, oh me,
Oh I will be your key,
Take care of trees,
Trees, oh trees.

Misty Bedford (9)
Abbey Park Primary School, Illingworth

Our Planet

Our planet needs nature,
It is major,
Nature is so good,
We really need mud and worms which are wiggly and tickly,
We need trees so we can have paper,
So we can draw birds later.

From robins and birds, we need more herbs,
From foxes to hedgehogs that hang around kerbs,
Grass needs some care, you need to be fair,
Come with me to find the frogs,
They're probably behind the logs,
Be happy for trees, they do good deeds, like helping us to breathe,
You shouldn't be mean.

Romily Ghani (9)
Abbey Park Primary School, Illingworth

A Wildcat

On this planet,
On the granite,
A creature stands tall.

No sign of happiness,
Its fur is like sappiness,
And it will bawl.

Because of the Earth it is distressed,
And its life has been messed,
So save the wildcats, save them all!

Their happiness grows,
As you help them dispose,
Dispose of their sadness,
Because their life is madness.

From big to small,
Save them all...

Olivia Flanagan (10)
Abbey Park Primary School, Illingworth

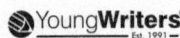

Our Planet Earth

Our planet Earth is a very special place,
From one country to another,
But some people make it a very big disgrace,
Our planet gets looked after by some,
Some people just act dumb.
I always feel bad for the trees,
Just swaying in the air,
I pray to them every night and hope they do repair.
People are just so heartless,
And it feels like nobody even cares,
But deep down I know everyone can't bare.

Myla McCallion (10)
Abbey Park Primary School, Illingworth

Earth And Nature

O ur community makes us safe
U nited lives
R eunion

E nvironment is kind
A ir is more important than you think
R eefs are where fish can keep safe
T hink about our planet
H elp our Earth

N ature is good for us
A irfare
T rees give us oxygen
U nite
R unning is healthy
E arth is our life.

Jasmine Mahmood (10)

Abbey Park Primary School, Illingworth

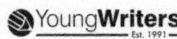

Ladybugs' Life

L ife is beautiful

A nimals are life forever

D amp weather is very bad for ladybugs as they can't fly then

Y affle, a yaffle is a type of woodpecker bird

B ushes are ladybugs' home and their life

U rchins are sea animals that have the sting of a jellyfish

G orgeous life beautiful nature, what could be better?

S moking is bad, and vapes.

Eliza Bates (10)

Abbey Park Primary School, Illingworth

My Earth Poem

C are for our planet
L et trees grow
I t is starting to get worse
M ore people are littering
A nimals are dying
T he Earth is crying
E normous tsunamis

C are for our trees
H ave care for our planet
A nimals are extinct
N ever litter
G et more help
E veryone needs to save the planet.

Jacob Sunderland (9)
Abbey Park Primary School, Illingworth

Wildlife

W arm coats from animals' skins are bad
I n their eyes, humans are mad
L ots of animals die every day
D aily we eat them, we eat them all day
L ots of trees get cut down daily
I n order to let us write away
F orest animals have a meaning too
E very bird constantly screeching.

Noah Pearmain (10)

Abbey Park Primary School, Illingworth

Trees, Bees, Butterflies And More Trees

The buzzing bees
The leaves on the trees
We don't see their hurt
Because the birds can only chirp
We love them all
We don't see their hurt
Trees give us oxygen
They die every day
And they don't do it their own way
We need to stay away
We need to stop
Or else they will rot.

Daisy Lewis (10)
Abbey Park Primary School, Illingworth

The Planet

To animals, our planet is scary and wild
But to us it's nice and mild
If a fox was all alone
We would ignore it and go
We need wildlife
We need to let it grow
Save the turtles some say
And stop pollution
Stop climate change
Be a climate champion today
And bring peace to our planet.

Mason Fenton (10)
Abbey Park Primary School, Illingworth

Our Earth

O wls hooting
U nder the sea there are beautiful fish swimming
R hinos stomping away

E arth is great
A nimals came in the early days
R ocks are good for skimming on the sea
T rees are life
H akuna Matata, like Pumbaa would say.

Ollie Maguire (10)
Abbey Park Primary School, Illingworth

Our Planet Earth

O cean
U K
R ivers

P lanet
L ove
A ble to do it
N ature
E nvironment
T rees

E arth
A rt
R espect
T ogether
H ope.

Harrison Challoner (10)

Abbey Park Primary School, Illingworth

Mother Nature

Nature, nature, oh Mother Nature
People in this world have got to mature
Leaving leaves, bees and trees to die
Can make a future you may not foresee
Air pollution can have no resolution
Although, we may turn this into a revolution!

Rylan Bedford (11)
Abbey Park Primary School, Illingworth

The Wild Running Animal

The wild running animal takes giant strides,
It climbs across the tall mountains,
And swims in the deep dark oceans,
Stomps across the lime-green grasses,
Over and over again.

The wild running animal is the strongest of them all,
He is the fastest,
The coolest of everyone around,
The wild running animal is unstoppable,
The wild running animal is unbeatable.

He is fast,
He is strong,
He is incredible,
He saves lives,
He is the humans' favourite.

The wild running animal loves the world,
Cares for everyone and has lived for years,
The wild running animal is an unbeatable, infinity deer.

Mila Woodall (9)
Glynne Primary School, Kingswinford

The Sleepy Gecko

In the depths of the forest, lived a gecko called
Jasper,
Jasper had a problem, he couldn't get to sleep,
So Jasper asked a tiger to tell the other animals to
be quiet,
But they didn't listen,
So Jasper asked the turtle to tell the animals to be
quiet,
But he was too slow,
So Jasper asked a bird to tell them to be quiet,
But he kept crashing into trees,
So the gecko asked the elephant to tell the others
to be quiet,
But the elephant made more noise,
So the last animal (the lion) asked the animals to
be quiet,
But for some reason he ate them all.
Finally, the gecko got some sleep.

William Baker (9)
Glynne Primary School, Kingswinford

The Running Deer's Escape

The deer runs at lightning speed
Escapes from predators very near
Runs through grass, leaves and plants
Badgers and foxes digging their homes.

Birds are nesting, ready for spring
All is calm around them
But the running deer still runs
Out of breath, she stops beside the great oak tree.

The animals keep going, determined
The running deer knows their strategy
She jumps over trees that fell in the wind
Until she comes to the deepest, darkest cave...

Jessica Pearson (9)
Glynne Primary School, Kingswinford

Save The Planet, Do Your Part

Save the planet,
You can help by remembering to recycle,
Or ride your bicycle,
Animals aren't the only thing that might go extinct,
Trees too.

Be careful, the Earth isn't renewable.

Don't chuck plastic in the ocean,
For the animals it's like a killing potion,
Their dreams will go to nothing,
If it was you, you would be blushing.

Be careful, the Earth isn't renewable.

Sam Kirkham (10)
Glynne Primary School, Kingswinford

The Rainforest

Down in the depths of the rainforest,
Lie branches dying,
Leaves decaying,
Branches falling from above.
Whilst before, there were lush green trees,
Trunks growing,
Vines criss-crossing everywhere,
Where it all used to be,
All green and full of different fruit,
And different animals.

Olivia Ball (9)
Glynne Primary School, Kingswinford

In The Woods

All I hear are the birds chirping and leaves rustling.
All I see are the birds flying over me.
All I feel is the breeze on my back.
Blackberries are growing on the bushes.

Ruby Cash (9)
Glynne Primary School, Kingswinford

YoungWriters® Est. 1991

Nature

We have to keep nature clean,
If we don't we're not going to have clean air anymore,
We have to care about nature,
Even if we don't want to,
Don't throw litter outside,
Put it in the bin,
There are some rules:
Remember, every little helps,
Don't throw litter in any zone,
Don't pollute the environment,
Clean nature to help her,
Give water to the trees.
We don't throw litter anywhere,
In hotels, in houses,
Outside, in parks,
Not even your own house.
If you see something,
Pick it up and put it in the bin.

We have to help nature as much as we can,
Because she is very big.
Also, don't throw litter in the water.

Cristina Trofin (9)
Lings Primary School, Lings

Save Our Planet

Protect, save the environment,
Someone make some movement,
Nature is what we need,
Let's all do something about it please.
Life moved faster every day,
If you don't know what that means, we don't have
any time to play,
Chaos and trouble around the world,
Take this seriously before it gets old.
Rubbish and trash stranded in the sea,
Don't mess around as you can see,
Turtles and fish need some help,
How would you feel if you were in this position?
It probably isn't your vision.
If you're dreaming, snap out of it quick,
Before everyone gets sick.

Ayan Sadik (11)
Lings Primary School, Lings

Saving The Environment!

Our environment is full of wonderful things,
Loads of plants and animals,
But that is all being ruined by the amount of
pollution in the world,
How much plastic is being left everywhere,
And how there is so much climate change.
My dream is to save the world,
And that animals are free to live without losing
their homes.
When I'm older, I'm going to discover how to fix
the amount of plastic being thrown everywhere,
And make sure everyone reduces, reuses and
recycles.
I am also going to reduce the amount of pollution.
Remember to take care of the environment!

Kaya Francis (9)
Lings Primary School, Lings

Bright Blue Beautiful Fish

When you use a straw or carry a plastic bag,
Do you think this makes fish happy, do you think it makes fish glad?
Fish in the North Pacific ocean eat 12,000 tonnes of plastic a year,
Think about this, doesn't this make you wish we could interfere?
Bright blue healthy fish are good for the environment,
We don't want to make them sick,
Or make them die too quick,
Oil is so bad,
Another problem we have that makes them sad,
Pollution, pollution,
We need to save the fishes!

Khayrat Abou (10)
Lings Primary School, Lings

Member Of The Genus Panthera

It's just my point of view,
Earth has beautiful nature.
I run very fast, 80km an hour,
But the climate is changing even faster.
I live on two continents.
I think that climate change and plastic pollution are problems for our entire planet.
Everyone needs protection and help from people,
Therefore, people should begin to recycle waste more.
I have a dream that we will all save our environment and take care of each other.
Now, you know who I am.

Answer: A jaguar.

Daniil Frunza (7)
Lings Primary School, Lings

25

The Endangered Axolotls

Down in the canals of Lake Xochimilco
In the sweet city of Mexico
There's a little problem you need to know.

You might be lucky enough
To be able to see
An axolotl.

With no more than a few hundred left in the wild
Sadly their species is becoming very mild
But they're very cute, would you want to raise an axolotl child?

Copper, leucistic, wild and gold
Let the mysteries of the axolotl unfold
There are just so many stories to be told!

Jessica Allen (10)
Lings Primary School, Lings

Foxes

Flocks fly to the east in the morning light,
Foxes show up in the gloomy night.
Foxes find prey,
And eat it all the way.
They have orange fur,
And love to lure.

They swish their tails,
And have long nails!
They like to play,
And also lay.
They love to eat,
Which is never neat.

Foxes live alone,
And always chew on bones!
Hunters rage,
When foxes run away.
They love to lie,
That's what they do in their lives.

Valerija Litinskaja (11)
Lings Primary School, Lings

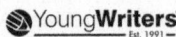

Summer Is The Best!

S miling all day long
U mbrellas away
M ore fun on the beach
M ore going out to play football
E ating ice cream all day long
R espectful and kind to your elders as we

H ave fun
O h no, did you get sunburnt?
L ick some ice cream all day
I t will pay
D ancing on Just Dance
A s we sing and play
Y ou should love the holiday.

Ryder Lambert (11)
Lings Primary School, Lings

The Big Green Poetry Machine

Recycling is good for the environment
If you don't recycle you're wasting
Also, you can junk to build fun things
Like making a robot costume out of cardboard boxes.
If you pick up trash you are a good person
You are helping the environment
If you are, thanks a lot
People leaving junk on the street is unacceptable
Especially in the sea
Leaving junk in the sea causes sea animals to die
So please don't.

Leonard Cigoreanu (8)
Lings Primary School, Lings

All About Our Planet

O ur planet is large
U nderwater can be found an exotic life
R ubbish damages our planet

P lants give us fresh air
L ands can be colourful and bright
A nimals can be found all over the planet
N ature can save people's lives
E nvironment needs to be protected by our generation
T rees are like our friends, they make the environment green and give us fruit.

Fabian Popa (7)
Lings Primary School, Lings

The Cold Winter

The fluffy red squirrel is hunting for nuts,
The kids are having fun in the snow,
The hares are boxing in the snow,
The leaves are crunchy in winter,
The kids are building a snowman,
The snow is getting heavier,
The kids are cold outside,
The animals are cold,
The pretty snowdrops are rising up,
The snowdrops live through the winter,
The people are warm inside,
The snow is dropping off the trees.

Avah-Renai Johnson (5)

Lings Primary School, Lings

Dirty Rivers

D irty rivers are not good
I f you see a dirty river, try to clean it up
R emember to be safe though!
T hank you, if you do clean it
Y ou don't have to though

R emember to be kind to Earth
I t will help the Earth!
V andalising rivers will not help Earth
E arth is a good place
R ivers are suffering from what we do
S top this!

Caleb Collins (11)

Lings Primary School, Lings

Save The Polar Bears

Polar bears are rare
Polar bears are white
We need to give them the rights
To have a happy home
And a place to roam.

Polar bears have a life
Children and a wife!
The ice is melting
We're leaving them stranded
We give them litter
How fair is this?
Polar bears
We need to save them
We need to stop littering
If you care about bears
Help these white bears too.

Erin Kenny (11)
Lings Primary School, Lings

My Special Summer

Summer breeze
Summer long
I'll sing to you
My summer song.

Read my poem
A summer song
It isn't long
It's just a song.

From my heart
A poem long
But not at all
My summer song.

My summer song
Is something special
A poem, a song
To my heart belong.

Summer breeze
Summer long

I'll sing to you
My summer song.

Andreea Bulancea (9)

Lings Primary School, Lings

There Is Nothing Greater

There is nothing greater
Than seeing animals in nature
There is nothing greater
Than seeing animals in water
There is nothing greater
Than seeing animals playing in the backyard
There is nothing greater
Than seeing animals dancing and prancing around
There is nothing greater
Than feeding the birds at the door
They always want more on the garden floor.

There is nothing greater...

Marley Rose (9)
Lings Primary School, Lings

The Monsters

When we come, you cower,
Scared what we can do,
With our big claws, our noise,
Drums right through you.

We don't care if it's your home,
Or you won't be able to breathe,
It doesn't really matter to us,
You don't need these trees.

Chop! Thunk! Crash!
The trees fall to the ground,
But we roll our eyes, turn our heads,
And leave without a sound.

Iola Welch (10)
Lings Primary School, Lings

Our World

Wonders of nature are right in our hands,
And before you know it,
It disappears like sand.

Flowers and plants bloom around us,
But they go out of existence,
We've had enough!

We want our trees to grow strong,
And making them fade,
It is quite wrong!

Let's team up and change our dear Earth,
Because it is disappearing,
And will have an impact on us!

Karolina Valanciute (10)

Lings Primary School, Lings

Environment

E xtinction is a thing
N ot to be messed with
V icious like a crow
I 'm gonna make a show
R ecycle, reduce, reuse
O therwise you're hurting me
N ot to mess with, so you don't make a scene
M aking our future
E ternal suffering
N ot to mess with
T ake it seriously

Save... our... planet!

Zena Bittar (11)

Lings Primary School, Lings

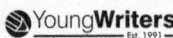

The Planet

T he Earth is ours to enjoy
H elp people to be happy
E very living thing is beautiful

P lanet Earth, my life, my home
L et's save trees and go green
A nimals and humans live together
N eptune is planet number eight
E arth is the only place for people to live
T his old Earth needs our help to stay fresh and clean.

Yanis Cocheci (7)
Lings Primary School, Lings

Earth's Problems

The Earth's problems are loads of things,
Like logging, pollution, endangered animals and
climate change.
Endangered animals like pandas, axolotls, rhinos,
elephants and tigers are nearly extinct.
Pollution is stuff like gases, cars and vapes,
They cause pollution which is bad for Earth.
Logging is bad since we need trees for a breeze,
If we don't have trees, we will die.

Muhammad Asghar (10)
Lings Primary School, Lings

The Seasons Of The Year

Spring -
The great warm weather
The flowers are blossoming
Easter is coming!

Summer -
Amazing weather
The people going outside
The whole Earth is great.

Autumn -
Going back to school
Pumpkins being harvested
The leaves are falling!

Winter -
Cold, snowy weather
Put your warm, fuzzy coats on
The leaves have fallen.

Samveer Singh (9)
Lings Primary School, Lings

A Tree Of Many Seasons

Spring -
My branches are coming to life,
My leaves are starting to grow.

Summer -
My leaves are very green,
But I need lots of water to grow.

Autumn -
My leaves are changing colour as it gets colder,
My branches are becoming bare.

Winter -
My leaves are all gone and my branches are totally bare,
It is far too cold to be out there.

James Keeber (10)
Lings Primary School, Lings

Littered Sea

The ocean has litter as we see,
Disturbing all the creatures in the sea.
We don't want to end their lives,
We don't want to say goodbye.
So we need to stop this, can you try?
We have turtles that we see,
All the bags that flee.
The ocean has litter as you see,
It's not that hard to recycle, don't you know?
Why can't we go back to 1933?

Lacey Massey (10)
Lings Primary School, Lings

Jake The Pirate And The Sea Monster

Jake the pirate was sailing on the sea
Along came a sea monster and grabbed him by the knee
Jake fell into the sea with a splash
"Oh no," said Jake, "look at all that rubbish!"

The monster wanted to show him all the mess
Jake looked at his fishing nets
And tidied some of the mess in the sea
"Thank you," said the sea monster.

Jake Skelton (8)
Lings Primary School, Lings

The World Needs Help!

Littering is bad,
With animals being sad.
People don't understand,
That vaping is terrible,
Smoking is horrible,
And animals are vanishing.
The world is crumbling in our hands.
Manhandling it like we own it,
Treating it like it's a dark pit.
Thank you Earth for letting us have a life,
And showing me the light.
I love you Earth.

Orlagh Malka (10)
Lings Primary School, Lings

Animals In Their Habitats

A pologies if I concern you but this cannot go on

N o more animals can die, it is very wrong

I f you litter, then animals eat it and die

M y heart then breaks and makes me cry

A nimals help the Earth, we need to help them survive

L ots of people depend on animals or we might not stay alive

S ave animals!

Olivia Higgs (9)
Lings Primary School, Lings

The Amazon

The Amazon is a pure green forest
Snakes slither around trees
Birds eat insects that have landed on green leaves.

The river is slow
But when you get to the heart it goes faster
There are lots of different kinds of fish in the river
The green lily pads float on the water
Frogs jump from lily pad to lily pad to play in the
bright sun.

Nathanael Marsh (7)
Lings Primary School, Lings

Bullies!

One day at school,
There was a new boy called Tommy,
The bullies were a girl called Belladax and her
friends.
First, they pushed him,
Then it happened again, again and again,
Until he told the teacher.
The teacher said, "Okay, I'll sort it out."
But she didn't tell her off,
Because she was her daughter.

Vaidehi Vadher (7)
Lings Primary School, Lings

Helping Earth

O ur planet is beautiful

U mbrellas keep us dry n the rain

R ain helps our plants to grow

P lease stop

L ittering, it is bad to litter

A t the woods, my brother fell over

N ot looking after our planet is bad

E arth has beautiful flowers

T rees help us breathe,

Kai Kelly (7)

Lings Primary School, Lings

Plastic

Sealife is in danger!
Plastic is in the sea,
The bad thing is that animals sometimes think it's food,
But instead it's a trap!
We need to start recycling,
It's better for the Earth,
Climate change is starting,
There's nothing else to do,
But the thing we must do is recycle,
And you can help us too!

Ella-Rae Bolton (9)
Lings Primary School, Lings

Earth

P lease keep our planet clean.

O pen your eyes and keep our world safe.

L eave your house and go outside.

L ove our planet.

U se water carefully.

T rees are vital to life.

I see the future Earth being clean.

O n our planet, I see fun.

N ever litter in our world.

Martina Aggrey (9)
Lings Primary School, Lings

Animals And Seasons

Roaming through the forest living their best life
Hunting for food in the middle of the night
Getting in your way, making a mess
Getting hit by people, there goes the fly for now.

Day and night, summer and winter
All the weathers mixed together
Snow and wind, lightning and thunder
Some are happy, some are not.

Sian Nurse (11)
Lings Primary School, Lings

The Life Of A Tree

Look at me,
I'm just a tree,
Living out my life,
In the luscious green.

I'm part of nature,
See you later,
I might just end up,
Your piece of paper.

People cut me down,
Making a lot of sounds,
Destroying the peace,
Spare me please,
Stop cutting me down with such ease!

Sean Mcgannon (11)
Lings Primary School, Lings

The Green Machine

The big, green, magical poetry machine,
With big, pink, glittery eyes,
Saw a big, orange tiger in the magical, animal,
poetry forest,
Holding a small, gold, frog coin.
The big tiger put the gold coin in the machine's
pink, glittery eyes,
Then they both lit up gold with glitter,
And they told poems to each other.

Tyesha Puta (6)
Lings Primary School, Lings

Happy Winter Day!

W hite frost on cupcakes
I cebergs
N arrow snowmen
T ime ticking for getting nice warm hot chocolate
E xtra cold winter
R otten snow, not to drink

D eforestation needs to stop
A good change for the environment
Y es, you can get a chance.

Nawal Kamal (8)

Lings Primary School, Lings

The Planet

We know that our planet is sick but not flat,
I know that in our world, there are lots of things.
I think we can build a home.
When we are in school on a Friday,
It is the last day.
TV is not real life,
But paper is from the trees,
And you can write on it with pens.
The moon is big in space now.

Danislava Pavlova (6)
Lings Primary School, Lings

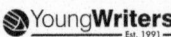

Wildlife

W ildlife is all around,
  I n the trees and on the ground,
  L eaves rustle while bunnies play,
D ogs and cats run away
  L ittle mice squeak and squirt,
  I n the fields animals get hurt,
  F urry animals go to sleep at night,
  E veryone is in bed all tight.

Michelle Benchea (10)

Lings Primary School, Lings

Sports!

Sports are good, sports are fun,
Sports are good for everyone.
You do sports, I do too,
Let's play together, me and you!
Sports is me, it might be you,
Do you like sports?
Because I certainly do!
Sports are cool, sports are fun,
Just to remind you,
They're here for everyone.

Khymari Donegal (10)
Lings Primary School, Lings

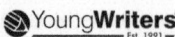

The Planet

T he Earth is gigantic
H earing the birds tweet is pretty
E ating gives you energy

P eople keep dropping
L itter
A nimals can be small or big
N ow there are no dinosaurs
E ating healthy is good
T aking medicine you should do.

Cassius King (6)
Lings Primary School, Lings

Stop Pollution!

Pollution is hurting our trees,
Hurting even the fleas,
Just because of human factories!
Smoke from houses can hurt our grass,
And we are losing flowers so enjoy the last,
Trees rotting and falling down really fast,
Not all humans are doing this,
So in our minds let's hope and wish.

Emilija Valanciute (10)
Lings Primary School, Lings

The Exploding Volcanoes

V olcanoes are dangerous
O ne volcano is exploding
L ives have to be saved
C an these people never go near volcanoes
A ll magma comes out and then there's ash
N o people archaeologists go to volcanoes
O n the volcano ash starts going down...

Mark Petrusevicius (8)

Lings Primary School, Lings

A Winter's Day

The snow is falling from the sky,
The flowers are covered in snow,
Let's go watch hockey,
Let's have a snowball fight,
Make snow angels and drink hot chocolate,
Squirrels run, looking for nuts,
The hares have snowball fights in the winter,
And the birds gather together.

Harrison Whitestone (5)

Lings Primary School, Lings

In The Ocean

In the ocean, crabs are small,
Whales are big and plants are tall.

In the ocean, it is bright,
Lots of colours glow at night.

In the ocean, a mermaid swam,
I want to meet her, I hope that I can.
In the ocean, I want to be,
Able to swim with dolphins and be free.

Ezmae Donegal (7)
Lings Primary School, Lings

Never Disrespect Nature

N ever disrespect nature because
A drop of water could one day save your life
T he trees provide oxygen to keep us alive
U nder the atmosphere you'll always be safe
R ivers flowing fresh and blue
E ver disrespect nature and you'll be sorry.

Priyal Karavadra (11)

Lings Primary School, Lings

Nature

N ature is everything you need,

A ll of the animals of the world help us,

T he world is wonderful, you see,

U se the useless things like plastic to create wonders,

R ecycling means we are going green,

E lectric also helps to stop polluting our air.

Maja Nicka (10)

Lings Primary School, Lings

Hundreds Of Us

Hundreds of houses, hundreds of homes,
Hundreds of mouses, hundreds of phones,
Hundreds of beds where I lay,
Hundreds of places where I stay,
Running, running, here and there,
Monday to Friday, I'm everywhere,
It's not that bad,
But oftentimes it makes me sad.

Alicija Gadaj (11)
Lings Primary School, Lings

Nature

N ature, there is nothing better
A s night falls it's as silent as an ant
T weets of beautiful birds as they stand on a tree branch
U p above the sun shines in delight
R obins and pigeons fly in the sky
E ast, where the sun tries to hide.

Eduard Atudorei (8)

Lings Primary School, Lings

Wildlife

W inter
I n winter the animals sleep
L ast winter wasn't so cold
D o you know what they are doing?
L ast night was snowy in the forest
I n summer it is so warm. What do you
F eel about it?
E verything you need.

Eva Pavlovecova (10)

Lings Primary School, Lings

The Snakes And The Animals In The Rainforest

There are so many animals in the rainforest,
Lots for you to see,
Like snakes and parrots,
Cheetahs and crocs,
Butterflies, monkeys,
And even frogs on logs!
There are so many there,
And plants to see,
Why don't you come to the rainforest with me?

Alfie Harte (6)
Lings Primary School, Lings

The Robin

One day a robin flew by
He came to our garden to say hi
He had a bright red breast
I like robins, they are the best
I hope he comes back for something to eat
Worms and seeds have been left as a treat
Come back and next time you will find something
to eat.

Archie Fox (7)

Lings Primary School, Lings

The Pain Of Modern-Day Shelters

Dogs, dogs, small, big, feisty and jumpy
Too many dying in horrible shelters
Not enough space, not enough kennels
For each dog to have sweet dreams
Each dog fearing to go into the door of no return
People try to hide this
But the truth is peeking through.

Esmai Wilson (11)
Lings Primary School, Lings

A Winter's Day

Let's build a snow house,
Snow is falling down.

Let's watch a nice game of ice hockey,
Snow is crunching.

Let's build a snowman,
Drink a hot chocolate.

Let's have a roast dinner,
And snuggle up in a blanket.

Harvey-Lee McKenzie (6)
Lings Primary School, Lings

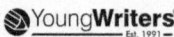

Don't Litter

Nature is full of life
And we don't want to hurt it
But people always litter
And it endangers animals.

The world needs our help
Because we are the cause of it
So stop it now and join me
Save the world and don't be the cause.

Aaron Dunkely (11)
Lings Primary School, Lings

Nature

N ature is such a delight
A nimals in the wilderness having fun
T rees dancing in the wind like a person
U nhappiness will never take over us
R oses blooming in the sunshine
E arth is a wonderful place to be!

Savanna Britton (9)
Lings Primary School, Lings

A Winter's Day

It's foggy and cold,
The wind is howling,
Put on your coats,
Let's go skating and skiing,
Drink a warm hot chocolate,
We can make snowmen and snow angels,
Have a snowball fight and go sledging,
Getting snuggly in my blanket.

Jasper Sharp (6)
Lings Primary School, Lings

Mother Nature

There is grass in this world
Please don't destroy it
Let's spread the word
Let's have a sit.

There are trees in this world
Please let's save them
Let's save this race
And Mother Nature's face.

Flourish Arifalo (11)
Lings Primary School, Lings

Spring Is Coming

Spring is coming, spring is coming,
The country is becoming green,
Sunflowers in the fields,
Let's all collect them.

Grow, grow, grass grow,
And the earth turns green,
Oh, I like her so much,
My dear spring.

Andreea Sterea (9)
Lings Primary School, Lings

Winter

The man built a snowman,
Hares were fighting and boxing,
Squirrels were eating - *crunch!*
In the soft snow in winter,
The bear walked up the mountain,
Penguins went down the mountain,
Penguins slid down the snow.

Artiom Adomnita (5)
Lings Primary School, Lings

Wildlife

Plant some trees
So you can be pleased
Live happily to the end of your days
Take it seriously all the time
No matter what comes in your way in life.

We need to stop animals from going extinct
And waving goodbye.

Ryan George (11)
Lings Primary School, Lings

Nature

N atural disasters happen
A nd nothing can stop them
T rees can break
U nderground will shake
R iver flow, but peacefully no more
E ven though it won't affect Earth's core.

Maja Cieslik (10)

Lings Primary School, Lings

Winter Kingdom

The rising snowdrops,
The penguins are sliding on the ice,
The bear climbs the tree,
The boxing hares,
The squirrel is nibbling,
The snow is cold,
The leaves are falling,
The people are building a snowman.

Ruby Wilson (6)
Lings Primary School, Lings

My Poem About Ronaldo, Messi And Neymar

Once there were 3 of the best footballers ever,
My personal favourite is Cristiano Ronaldo,
He loves animals and weather,
The cool thing about Neymar and Ronaldo,
Is that they both have the same birthday, 5th
February.

Ryley Kelly (9)
Lings Primary School, Lings

The Earth Poem

The grass is green,
The rocks are grey,
The sky is blue,
And I am okay.
This is a poem I like,
I might just spend my whole life,
I love the Earth, I love my life,
I'm done with my poem, bye-bye.

Penny Woods (7)
Lings Primary School, Lings

Once I Saw A Little Bird

Once I saw a little bird come and hop, hop, hop!
I cried, "Little bird, will you stop, stop, stop?"
I was going to the window to say, "How do you do?"
But he shook his little tail and away he flew.

Oyindamola Nuga (6)
Lings Primary School, Lings

A Winter's Day

Sledging down the hill,
And making snow angels,
It is freezing cold,
Put on your coat and scarf,
Snuggle in a blanket,
You can watch TV,
Put your boots on,
Jump in the snow and have fun.

Darcy Millar (5)
Lings Primary School, Lings

Winter

The fluffy brown birds are flying,
And they are looking for food,
The req squirrel is nibbling nuts,
The hares are boxing,
The animals are searching for food,
The people are building a snowman.

Gloria Nasonkina (5)

Lings Primary School, Lings

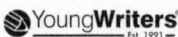

The Winter

People make a snowman,
With the fluffy snow in winter,
Leaves fall to the ground,
And they crunch!
The hares are boxing in the fluffy snow,
In the winter, sometimes there are rainbows.

Elliott York (5)

Lings Primary School, Lings

Seasons

Green grass grows,
Cold winds blow,
Bright blue sky,
Yellow sun shines,
Leaves falling off trees,
Flower pollen for bees,
Animals are sleeping,
After lots of eating.

Maddison-Amara Culhane (6)
Lings Primary School, Lings

A Winter's Day

Let's go skating and skiing,
Drink a hot chocolate,
Throw snowballs,
Make snow angels,
Have a piping hot roast dinner,
It's foggy and cold,
And the sky is grey.

Reginald Manu (6)
Lings Primary School, Lings

Save Our Planet

Please recycle, it will help
Pick up rubbish if you see it
We only have one Earth
Every person counts
Don't be one of those people that doesn't recycle
Be helpful!

Monica Allen (8)
Lings Primary School, Lings

Good Things About Water

W ater is all around us
A nimals live underwater
T urn off the tap to save water
E veryone needs water to live
R ivers travel around the world.

Leighton Mickenzie (9)

Lings Primary School, Lings

Saving Animals

Animals are so important!
Polar bears are white,
Crocodiles always want to fight,
Up high, you will see some butterflies,
Foxes, you only see when there's no light.

Nyla-Rose Lewis (8)
Lings Primary School, Lings

YoungWriters Est. 1991

A Winter's Day

Lots of fun fresh snow,
Looking at me,
It is gold and frosty.

Throwing snow at my teachers,
And laughing,
I can feel snowflakes,
On my hot hands.

Madalina Dorofei (5)
Lings Primary School, Lings

My Two Dogs

In their new house lives Nan and Pap
With their dogs Luna and Poppy
The dogs are big and black
We take them for a walk
They bark and they don't climb steps!

Niamh Mayhew (6)
Lings Primary School, Lings

What Is A Winter's Day Made Of?

The fluffy red squirrel,
Has fluff to keep warm,
The hares are boxing,
You make snowmen,
The trees are bare,
It is cold in the winter,
It is snowing.

Samuel Allen (5)
Lings Primary School, Lings

The Big And Beautiful Wolf

The big and beautiful wolf is very fierce
In the morning he goes out after food
To give him strength all day
He eats only meat
He has a very large appetite.

Dimitri Matran (8)
Lings Primary School, Lings

Earth

E veryone should look after the planet
A lways pick up litter
R ecycle leftovers
T urn off the lights
H elp us save the world.

Mia Murphy (8)
Lings Primary School, Lings

Winter

W inter holiday
I s fun
N ow it is
T ime to have some fun
E ating some food and
R oasting marshmallows.

Jaiden Clark (10)

Lings Primary School, Lings

About Winter

The red fox was hunting for food,
The squirrel was happy,
The snowdrops were rising up beautifully,
The winter was cold and the owls were flying.

Geon Gilin (6)

Lings Primary School, Lings

Winter Animals

The hares are boxing,
There are thousands of birds,
Animals looking for food,
People are building a snowman,
The bird is looking at the mud.

Jacob Franklin (6)
Lings Primary School, Lings

A Winter's Day

Making snow angels and throwing snowballs,
We can drink hot chocolate,
Jumping in the snow, let's build a snowman,
You can catch snowflakes.

Saphire-Ruby Garrett (6)
Lings Primary School, Lings

Who Am I?

A small sea creature
I walk very slow
I live in the sea
Sometimes I live on land
Who am I?

Answer: I am a sea turtle.

Chelsea Konadu (9)
Lings Primary School, Lings

The Fox

The fox hunts his prey,
And lives in a hole in the forest,
He runs around the forest,
That is massive,
And runs after the other animals.

Niamh Kenny (11)
Lings Primary School, Lings

A Winter's Day

It is snowing,
Drink hot chocolate,
Wear your coat,
You can make snow angels,
Snuggle up in a blanket,
You can make a snowman.

Ellie Burley (5)
Lings Primary School, Lings

Winter Season

Christmas shopping
Cake frosting
Snowball throwing
Present making
Ice skating
Tree decorating.

Stefania Rotaru (9)
Lings Primary School, Lings

A Winter's Day

The snow is falling down,
Snuggle up, nice and warm,
Make a snowman,
Enjoy a hot chocolate.

Zara Bittar (5)
Lings Primary School, Lings

Winter World

You build a snowman,
The squirrels search for nuts,
In the fluffy snow of this winter world.

Logan Rowland (6)

Lings Primary School, Lings

Ananconda Acrostic

G reen anacondas can grow up to 9 metres

R ed anacondas are a myth

E xactly, there are about 3 different species

E ver roaming the swamps and rivers of South America

N ever tangle with an anaconda because it will tangle with you!

A nacondas are the biggest type of snake in the Amazon

N ever born in trees

A re constricting snakes

C onstricting means they squeeze their prey until they can't breathe

O n the day they are born they are born in the water

N ever has someone survived an anaconda

D angerous reptile

A nacondas are my favourite snake.

James McClure (8)
McKinney Primary School, Dundrod

Snow Leopard

S now leopards are colourful and bright animals.

N ever easy to spot.

O n the ice all day long, playing in the snow.

W ild deer in the snow ready to eat.

L ovely soft fur, so warm and cosy.

E ver hunted for my fur.

O n the vulnerable animal list I sit.

P redator of the Himalayas.

A lways very fast.

R eally good at camouflage.

D welling in my den with my cubs.

Luxie Milliken (8)

McKinney Primary School, Dundrod

Snow Leopards

S now leopards live on snowy mountains
N early snow leopards are extinct
O ver the Himalayas I run free
W ild deer in the snow, ready to eat

L ovely soft fur, so warm and cosy
E ver hunted for fur
O h all animals deserve to live in peace
P lease protect us
A lways very fast
R ight are snow leopards, wrong are people
D isguising myself is my best skill.

Olly Jay (8)
McKinney Primary School, Dundrod

YoungWriters®
Est. 1991

Oceans Acrostic Poem

O h, please don't throw rubbish, I pray, you are killing my fish every day.

C ome and put rubbish in the bin, you pollute me. Meanies!

E asygoing, don't pollute me. Put rubbish in the bin!

A hh, my dear old friends, fish and shark, whale and squid. Help them quick!

N ow put rubbish in the bin, you are killing my friends.

S ave our oceans!

Julianne Craig (7)
McKinney Primary School, Dundrod

What Am I?

I am a sphere.
I am one of the planets.
I am mostly blue and green.
People call me the Blue Planet.
I have one moon.
Humans build houses and schools on me.
The wind cools me off.
The plants and flowers are a part of me.
Lots of humans and animals call me home.
What am I?

Answer: I am the Earth.

Lexi Bryans (8)
McKinney Primary School, Dundrod

Reindeer

Our rainforest is the most beautiful rainforest in the world.
The reindeer eat grass, mosses, leaves, herbs and ferns in the forest every day.
The reindeer live in the forest, they love playing around the forest.
Reindeer like to run and play about in the rainforest.
The reindeer go with Santa.

Chloe Watson (7)
McKinney Primary School, Dundrod

Arctic Fox

A rctic foxes looking for food
R ound Arctic woods
C areful
T hey have to go quick
I ce is melting
C racking, especially in summer.

F ast as 31mph
O ver the hills they go.
X anthophore means a cold-blooded animal.

Anna Nicholson (7)
McKinney Primary School, Dundrod

Birds Acrostic

B e kinder to birds in the winter because they have no food.

I love parrots because they are lovely and colourful.

R aptors are persecuted for human greed, cruel humans.

D inosaurs are my closest relative.

S weet, singing, hummingbirds in the Amazon.

Priscilla Bell (7)

McKinney Primary School, Dundrod

The Ocean

O h, stop putting rubbish in my home.
C rabs, dolphins, whales and fish call me home.
E verlasting source of life.
A nimals live in me, please be careful.
N one of my animals like it when you litter in their home.
S ave our oceans!

Maisie Bamford (8)

McKinney Primary School, Dundrod

Peacock Acrostic

P eacocks are colourful.
E xcited exhibitionist.
A lways being a show-off.
C lever!
O ften they are prancing.
C areful taking care of my chicks.
K ept in Indian gardens for princesses.

Evie Minford (8)

McKinney Primary School, Dundrod

Rainforest

I am warm, colourful, rainy and humid.
Humans cut down my trees.
I am home to many different creatures.
Trees, rivers and plants are all part of me.
Animals lose their homes because of toxic human greed.
I am a rainforest.

Matthew Flanagan (7)
McKinney Primary School, Dundrod

What Am I?

I live in the sea.
I'm the biggest animal on the planet.
I'm endangered.
I'm a mammal.
I eat plankton and fish.
I'm a gentle giant.
What am I?

Answer: I'm a blue whale.

Nate Dawson (8)
McKinney Primary School, Dundrod

Sloths

S loths slowly moving through the trees.
L ovely, cuddly animal.
O h, stop cutting down my home.
T rees are where I belong.
H ear them crying from the trees.
S ave the sloths.

Coleen Harbinson (8)

McKinney Primary School, Dundrod

What Am I?

Oh help from the rubbish.
Clean my waters.
Help me and my animal friends.
Every day, I see rubbish.
Please clean my water.
Never litter on the beach.
What am I?

Answer: I am the ocean.

Luke Montgomery (8)
McKinney Primary School, Dundrod

What Am I?

I am bright and colourful.
I live near the Amazon river.
I'm very dangerous, people use me to hunt.
I'm very small.
Do not go near me.
What am I?

Answer I am a poison dart frog.

Harrison Brown (8)
McKinney Primary School, Dundrod

The Ocean

O rcas, octopuses, whales and dolphins call me home.

C lean the ocean.

E xtreme pollution endangers my animals.

A lways keep plastic away from me.

N ever litter on the beach.

Ryan Duckett (8)

McKinney Primary School, Dundrod

Koala Acrostic

K eep us safe from forest fires.

O ur trees are burning down.

A ll our eucalyptus is ruined!

L ovely, cute marsupials.

A s endangered as can be.

S ave the koalas!

Martha Dunlop (8)

McKinney Primary School, Dundrod

Riddle Poem

I have black spots, but mostly yellow.
I am very fast like a bullet.
Hunter of the savannah.
I am hunted for my fur.
Please leave me in peace.
What am I?

Answer: I am a cheetah.

Charlotte Brown (7)
McKinney Primary School, Dundrod

What Am I?

I am slow.
I have hair.
I like to eat leaves.
I squeak so my mum and dad can find me.
I sleep 15 hours a day.
Algae grows on my hair.
What am I?

Answer: I am a sloth.

Annie Gordon (7)
McKinney Primary School, Dundrod

Sloths

Their homes are being chopped down.
We shouldn't be doing that.
Sloths make a squeaky sound.
They sleep for over 15 hours!
They live in forests and trees.
Lovely slow-as-a-snail sloths!

Flynn Allison (7)
McKinney Primary School, Dundrod

What Am I?

I live in the forest.
I've got brown skin.
I live in trees.
I eat bananas.
I have a long tail.
I live in groups.
What am I?

Answer: I am a monkey.

Lewis Park (7)
McKinney Primary School, Dundrod

The Rainforest

I am warm, colourful and rainy.
I am home to many different creatures.
Trees, rivers and plants are all part of me.
Humans cut down my trees.
I wish my animals could be safe.

Dawson Baker (8)
McKinney Primary School, Dundrod

Deforestation

D o not destroy animals' homes
E ven all the different biomes
F ellow people are chopping wood
O ur people are misunderstood
R esources are less
E ndangering wood is not good
S top it and go towards success
T ry to protect the tropical environment
A nd get your eco-friendly degrees
T ry to plant more trees
I nclude others and get your entitlement
O ngoing should be our beautiful wilderness
N ow we are filled with love and kindness

Zahra Shahbaz (8)
Sacred Heart RC Primary School, Blackburn

We Like Earth

We are Year 4
We need to say and do a lot more
We need to be green,
To keep the Earth clean.
Don't make more cars,
They suffocate the Earth with harmful gas.
Grow more plants,
And do a happy dance.
Put rubbish in the bin,
Like tins or other things.
Look after water,
Life without it is a lot shorter.
Water is cool,
We drink it a lot at school.
Water is blue,
It can be cold or warm too.
It is very refreshing in hot weather,
It feels like a soft feather.
Look after the air we breathe,
Without it the Earth is dead.

Learn to keep air clean,
Don't be mean.
Air is good,
Just like it should.
Even if you are 3,
Look after the air, like me.
We like animals,
We are mammals.
Look at our playground,
There are no plants to be found.
We are in the same world,
Most of the plants are curled.
We have to look after everything,
Like it is a valuable ring.
Look after fire,
It is something we should admire.
It could be bad,
You will get mad.
Fire can actually be bad and good,
It could get bigger, yes it could.
If it spreads call 999,
Then you will be fine.

You could have a barbecue,
Invite friends and family too.
Mammals give birth to a live baby,
Some on the ground, some in holes maybe.
Reptiles give birth to little eggs,
When they hatch some have little legs.
Nature is beautiful,
And very colourful.

Adela Dahdouh (9)
Sacred Heart RC Primary School, Blackburn

Here Comes Winter

H ot never allowed
E verything cold
R unning around all the animals in the cold
E verybody wearing warm clothes

C old everywhere
O ffering you the flu
M any things freeze
E ndless cold
S everal things freeze

W ind blowing everywhere
I cy the river is
N ice it feels in wooly clothes
T ea is nice in winter
E verywhere you look there's only snow
R ain melting things, but not this time.

Aisha Ashfaq (9)
Sacred Heart RC Primary School, Blackburn

Rainforest

R ain is important for plants and oxygen

A ir is important for plants and other things like humans

I f I don't cut down trees, then you don't cut down trees

N o polluting

F orests are dying because of paper

O xygen will be less if you cut down trees

R ainforests are our future

E veryone needs to look after the rainforests like I do

S ave the rainforests for the next generation

T ime is ticking, save the rainforests!

Atiya Zain Iqbal (8)
Sacred Heart RC Primary School, Blackburn

A Riddle

What am I?
I create destruction.
I kill people.
After people are done with me, families are miserable.
I can only stop with peace.
Creatures are killed because of me.
I got created by humans.
Humans can use me if there are lots of them wanting to attack others.
People can make alliances if there are other people.
People tried to stop me, but some failed during the process.
Peace is one of the solutions to stop me.
I am not a living creature or plant.

Aiza Hussain (9)
Sacred Heart RC Primary School, Blackburn

Rainforests Are Beautiful

R ain is good for our environment.
A nimals are good too.
I am kind to animals so you should be too.
N ever cut down trees.
F orests are getting cut down.
O n the Earth there are endangered animals.
R emember, animals live here too.
E els are kinder than you think.
S piders are nice too.
T he Earth needs to be taken care of.

Aira Kashif (8)
Sacred Heart RC Primary School, Blackburn

Wildlife

W ildlife is amazing.

I nsects crawl around leaves and branches.

L ive happily amongst animals, creatures and our wildlife.

D ifferent species surround each other.

L iving creatures are everywhere.

I n green forests amazing animals live or die.

F orests and oceans... they are all important.

E veryone should help protect the wildlife.

Ziya Patel (9)

Sacred Heart RC Primary School, Blackburn

Eco System

E verybody needs to care for our nature and elements

C an we do it?

O f course, we have to recycle

S o much nature we are given

Y ou have to help

S everal reasons why we should take care

T oo many animals might go extinct

E co system is fragile

M any animals are having a hard time surviving.

Aleena Kamal (8)
Sacred Heart RC Primary School, Blackburn

What Is It?

It's rainy, it's wet
On the ground it is a very good habitat for animals
The environment for trees is really bad
You cannot walk around it
It is part of Brazil
Starts with an 'R'
What is it?
Did you guess?

Answer: It's the rainforest.

Eryka Aldea (9)
Sacred Heart RC Primary School, Blackburn

Water

W ater is good because it is refreshing

A nd fish can live in water, they have

T ails to help them swim well, this is because fish like water

E ven they can die if they are not in the water

R un or a shark can kill you if you are very far from the beach.

Adam Mohamed (8)

Sacred Heart RC Primary School, Blackburn

Riddle Poem

I am in your sleep
Sometimes you're scared of me
Sometimes you want me to be real
There are clouds around me
You're in bed
I am not real
You also might be confused where you are
What am I?

Answer: I am a dream.

Ummay Fatima Bhatti (9)
Sacred Heart RC Primary School, Blackburn

What Am I?

I can burn
I can melt iron
I can burn your skin
I can burn trees
You use me for warming
You use me for cooking
Sometimes I am dangerous
Sometimes I am helpful
What am I?

Answer: I am fire.

Amalia Nasukhanova (9)
Sacred Heart RC Primary School, Blackburn

Riddle

I am outside all the time
I like the sun
I don't like the cold
I am tall
I can be any colour
People see me all the time
I am in people's homes
What am I?

Answer: Flowers.

Rukaia Ibrahim (9)
Sacred Heart RC Primary School, Blackburn

Protect Our World

Two roads, side by side
Which one would you rather ride?
The road with the toads, lions and toucans
Or the road with all the rich people and no
animals?
The road with caves, waves and a beach
Or the road with the traffic and tyres that screech?
The road with the trees and the bumblebees
Or the polluted road that smells like cheese?
If you want to travel on the road with the sea
You need to consider how you're going to be
Recycle your rubbish, turn out the light
And keep our world looking bright.

Elliott Gardner (8)
Somerset Bridge Primary School, Bridgwater

Our Planet

O ut of the world
U nderstand the danger
R espect the world/planet

P rotect the environment
L ife for all of us could be saved
A lways recycle
N ever litter
E arth is our only home
T rees need to be planted not cut.

Kristian Wheeler (7)
Somerset Bridge Primary School, Bridgwater

Trees

T rees are important
R etrieve oxygen from them
E very day they keep us alive
E nd this disaster
S ave the trees.

Florence Bunce (8)

Somerset Bridge Primary School, Bridgwater

Save The World!

A kennings poem

Tree planter
Animal cuddler
Sea saver
Habitat maker
Path walker
Daily recycler
World hunger ender
Animal helper
Nature protector
Road renewer
World protector.

Callum Naylor (10)

St Cuthbert's Catholic Primary School, Walbottle Village

People Who Are Ruining The World!

A kennings poem

Sea polluter
Habitat destroyer
Animal pocher
Forest chopper
Factory owner
Zoo keeper
Skin shaver
Litter dropper
House builder
Ice melter
World breaker.

Nyle Hassan (9)

St Cuthbert's Catholic Primary School, Walbottle Village

Our World Right Now!

A kennings poem

Ice cap melter
Forest fire
Tree cutter
Animal hunter
Habitat ruiner
Vehicle driver
Skin shaver
Sea polluter
Litter spreader
Meat eater
World ender...

Ella Leddicoat (9)

St Cuthbert's Catholic Primary School, Walbottle Village

Global Warming

A kennings poem

Ice melter
Plastic dropper
Habitat demolisher
Tusk keeper
Air polluter
Factory spiller
Wood cutter
Forest destroyer
Car driver
Earth ender.

Alfie Daymond (10)

St Cuthbert's Catholic Primary School, Walbottle Village

Me

A kennings poem

Daily recycler
Path walker
Litter picker
Tree planter
Flora helper
Habitat keeper
Animal saver
Turtle breeder
Food giver
World lover.

Olivier Belzynski (9)
St Cuthbert's Catholic Primary School, Walbottle Village

YoungWriters®
Est. 1991

Save Our Earth!

A kennings poem

Tree planter
Animal feeder
Daily recycler
Litter picker
Flower planter
Path walker
Landfill collector
World helper
Mammal breeder.

Hamiz Khan (10)

St Cuthbert's Catholic Primary School, Walbottle Village

Me! Helping The World

A kennings poem

Path walker
Plant grower
Pollution stopper
Animal helper
Litter picker
Habitat saver
Food giver
Ocean maker
World saviour.

Gabriella Hewson (9)
St Cuthbert's Catholic Primary School, Walbottle Village

Save The World!

A kennings poem

Habitat maker
Tree planter
Pollution stopper
Path walker
Animal saver
Ice cooler
Litter binner
Sea lover
World saver.

Billy Doyle (10)
St Cuthbert's Catholic Primary School, Walbottle Village

Habitat Destroyer

Foxes' woodland
Gorillas' jungle
Rabbits' burrows
Crocodiles' swamps
Elephants' savannas
Habitat destroyer.

Amaan Qaiser (9)

St Cuthbert's Catholic Primary School, Walbottle Village

Global Warming!

A kennings poem

Acid lover
Habitat destroyer
Litter dropper
Tree ender
Truck driver
Animal hater
Landfill spiller
World shredder.

Eva Costigan (9)

St Cuthbert's Catholic Primary School, Walbottle Village

Planet Saver

A kennings poem

Path walker
Tree planter
Litter picker
Pollution stopper
Animal helper
Habitat creator
Food giver
World saver!

Rafay Ishaque (10)

St Cuthbert's Catholic Primary School, Walbottle Village

Global Warming Ender

A kennings poem

Path walker
Pollution stopper
Tree grower
Litter picker
Animal helper
Habitat creator
Food giver
World saver.

John Jennings (10)
St Cuthbert's Catholic Primary School, Walbottle Village

Save Our World

A kennings poem

Tree planter
Cold maker
Animal lover
Path walker
Litter picker
Sea cleaner
Landfill recycler
World saver.

Aleena Ismail (10)

St Cuthbert's Catholic Primary School, Walbottle Village

My Way Of Saving Our Planet

A kennings poem

Litter picker
Sea cleaner
Tree grower
Animal saver
Wildlife maker
Flora planter
Non polluter
World saver.

Robson Doyle (9)
St Cuthbert's Catholic Primary School, Walbottle Village

Save Our World

A kennings poem

Tree grower
Litter picker
Path walker
Habitat lover
Animal helper
Food giver
Daily recycler
World saver.

Heidi Blackett (9)

St Cuthbert's Catholic Primary School, Walbottle Village

What You Should Stop!

A kennings poem

Ice breaker
Car driver
Turtle catcher
Litter lover
Planet destroyer
Tree chopper
Landfill spiller.

Amelia Hardy (9)

St Cuthbert's Catholic Primary School, Walbottle Village

How I Save The World

A kennings poem

Litter picker
Animal saver
Daily recycler
World lover
Habitat maker
People helper
Charity donator.

Jess Mciver (10)
St Cuthbert's Catholic Primary School, Walbottle Village

I Love My Planet

A kennings poem

Plant grower
Litter picker
Daily recycler
Animal saver
Charity donator
Tree needer
World lover.

Edward Dodgson (9)
St Cuthbert's Catholic Primary School, Walbottle Village

Could Be...

A kennings poem

Flora planter
Rubbish recycler
Litter picker
Sea saver
Habitat maker
Animal lover
World saver.

Maisie Rodelas (9)

St Cuthbert's Catholic Primary School, Walbottle Village

How To Save The Planet

A kennings poem

Sea cleaner
Litter picker
Animal saver
Tree planter
Animal picker
Landfill spiller
Word saver.

Alfie Gray (10)

St Cuthbert's Catholic Primary School, Walbottle Village

Saving The World

A kennings poem

Tree planter
Sea saver
Animal lover
Bike rider
Habitat maker
Litter picker
World saver.

Maria Khaliq (9)

St Cuthbert's Catholic Primary School, Walbottle Village

Animal Saver

Elephant tusk
Fish bag
Turtle saviour
Gorilla jungle
Monkey tail
Turtle straw.

Zaara Zafar (10)
St Cuthbert's Catholic Primary School, Walbottle Village

World Saver

A kennings poem

Tree planter
Animal helper
Recycle picker
Sea cleaner
Bike rider
World saver.

Husnain Jawed (10)
St Cuthbert's Catholic Primary School, Walbottle Village

Our World

A kennings poem

Litter picker
Tree planter
Path walker
Sea saver
Wildlife maker
World saver.

Francesca McRoberts (10)

St Cuthbert's Catholic Primary School, Walbottle Village

Why Animals Go Extinct

Turtle straw
Fish bag
Elephant tusk
Lion fur
Monkey trees
Animals extinct.

Beau Shearer (10)

St Cuthbert's Catholic Primary School, Walbottle Village

Save The Planet

A kennings poem

Plant planter
Sea cleaner
Rubbish picker
Bike rider
Planet helper.

Max Towns (9)

St Cuthbert's Catholic Primary School, Walbottle Village

Rainforest

R oots of a tree keep the tree alive.

A nimals in the rainforest are very intelligent.

I ndigo flowers are pretty and purple.

N aughty, cheeky monkeys swing from tree to tree.

F lying birds are very colourful and like to call.

O celots are very sneaky, watch out for them!

R ecycle all your rubbish so you keep the rainforest safe.

E merald tree boas are very green and blend in the trees.

S carlet macaws are very noisy, "Squawk!" they say.

T igers are very sneaky! Careful not to wake one by tickling its tail.

Leo Makzal (7)

St Joseph's Primary School, Gabalfa

Our Planet

O ur planet Earth is quite
U nique and special to people
R ound it goes, it orbits all year round

P eople enjoy all four seasons
L ittle bit of rain and little bit of sun
A nd with air we breathe thanks to all the trees
N eed to keep you clean for more people to come
E arth, what a beauty you are... full of nature
T ime to save our planet from pollution and litter.

Jumaima Uddin (7)
St Joseph's Primary School, Gabalfa

The Jungle Was Massive

I miss the time when all my family was around
We stood tall together
Now every time I open my eyes
My family are nowhere to be found
I used to see my friends playing
Animals brought me so much joy
It makes me sad their homes are gone
I want everyone to know how important we are
We are homes to animals
We bring fresh air to the planet
Me and my friends should be protected
For the future of the world.

Teddy Bowen (7)
St Joseph's Primary School, Gabalfa

Planet Earth

The Earth is big, the Earth is round
The Earth has trees and flowers all over the ground.
Skies are blue, the seas are deep
The Earth is a happy place to sleep.
The wind is strong, the sun is hot
We need to look after the planet we've got.

Jacob Williams (7)
St Joseph's Primary School, Gabalfa

Pakistan We Love You

Lands of green
Skies of blue
The people are great
With great love
Pakistan is united
Pakistan is one
The foods smell like heaven
Full of flavour
You are Pakistan
Pakistan is you.

Aadil Maghal (8)
St Joseph's Primary School, Gabalfa

Recycling

R ubbish

E arth

C limate change

Y ou should recycle

C an this go in the recycle bin?

L ove the

E nvironment.

Noah Diaz (8)

St Joseph's Primary School, Gabalfa

The Star

Oh almighty star
How I wonder what you are!
Deep in the depths of space and all
A mystery never solved
All in the deep, deep, deep...

Ire Balogun (8)
St Joseph's Primary School, Gabalfa

Chimpanzee

Here I am,
Here I wake,
I can see the sunlight shining through the leaves
I enjoy swinging through the trees as the Earth
breathes.
Birds pecking at the bark,
Creatures exploring the dark.
The river flowing,
The ripples glowing.
The forest is alive around me,
Oh, it's a joy to be free.

Suddenly!
The birds arise,
I can hear their cries.
The creatures start to stir,
And run around in a blur.
I'm scared!
I can hear strange noises,
Sounds like angry voices.
The sky becomes black with smoke,
An ever-growing cloak.

The trees start to fall,
As I recall.
I see two-legged creatures chopping at the tree
with evil intention,
With no intervention.
I run.
I'm chased.
I feel a sharp pain.
It goes dark.

I'm awake!
But I'm alone! Alone!
I let out a mighty groan,
A moan.
The creatures appear and come near.
They seem reactive to my calls,
But I already know I'm captive inside their walls.
A tyre to swing,
A bell to ring,
Food and water the creatures bring.
Time is repetitive and insensitive,
Oh, I don't like being me,
I want to be in my tree.

One day they come, but it's different,
And, unknown to me, it will be magnificent!
Again, it goes dark,
And on my long journey I embark.
I open my eyes,
I seem trapped inside a tree,
But a slither of light reaches towards me.
I hear an engine hum,
And drum.
The tumbling and turning stops,
And the door to the cage drops.
I'm blinded by the light,
But for some reason, I know it's going to be alright.
I hear the birds singing,
I can see creatures running,
And once again I can smell the sweet scent of the blossom trees.
Finally, I'm free,
Back to my home.

So, the message I bring,
Is stop this occurring!
Let us not cut down but sow,

And let the forest regrow.
Let its beauty show.
Let's stop deforestation!

Nikita Neverov (7)
The Elms Junior School, Long Eaton

Believe In Bears

B e hopeful for bears

E verywhere bears are suffering because of us

L ove bears however big or small

I ce caps and other areas are bears' homes, why destroy them?

E ven though they are far, they still matter

V ery sad for us to hear about bears, let's change that

E verybody can help, start now!

I nteract with climate change

N ever give up on bears

B ears have a life, let's make it a good one

E verybody cheer for bears

A nything will help, so help

R ights for bears

S ave bears!

Sophia Baldwin (9)

The Elms Junior School, Long Eaton

Porpoises And Me

P orpoises are dying because of us

O nly ten left, oh no!

R ight this wrong

P lease save them while you can!

O therwise they will be gone

I f we don't help now, they will die

S orrowful is the situation

E very day we do nothing they fight for their lives

S ometimes you just need to make a change and do something!

A nd now is the time

N ever should we give up now

D o something, you can help

M aybe if everyone helped, we could save them

E very second we are wasting they are dying!

Freya Baldwin (9)

The Elms Junior School, Long Eaton

Save Our Squirrels

S ciurus vulgaris is the Latin name for our native red squirrels

Q uite alarmingly red squirrels are disappearing

U nder threat of extinction from the grey squirrel

I ntroduced from America, the greys are taking over

R ed squirrels won't breed when stressed

R oad traffic and woodland loss are also factors in their decline

E ating them before the reds, the greys like the taste of under-ripe acorns

L ots of red squirrels die from a disease carried by the greys.

Heather Irving (8)

The Elms Junior School, Long Eaton

If I Was A Polar Bear!

If I was a polar bear,
I would live north of everywhere.
The polar bears are amazing,
They really need saving.
My fish keep on disappearing,
Because you humans keep on misbehaving.
Antarctica is melting and the planet is dying,
The world is in such sorrow,
Let's make a difference tomorrow.
If I was a polar bear,
I would snuggle up in my fur,
And roll in the snow everywhere.
Let's help our planet and let's change our ways,
To save our polar bears.

Mareck Yarlett (9)
The Elms Junior School, Long Eaton

Earth

Earth is our home
Our life
Our love
Earth is the trees
And the sky above
Earth we live on
It's given us birth
Look after the planet
The trees and the seas
The air and the flowers
The butterflies and bees
Look after the Earth
For generations to come
The children then will want to play and run
Don't harm our Earth
Never, ever
And care for our Earth
Forever and ever.

Avani Athwal (10)

The Elms Junior School, Long Eaton

Cheetah

C heetahs live in Africa

H umans sometimes kill these amazing cats

E xtinction could happen without our help

E yes have a black tear running down their face

T hey are so amazing, they can run 3m in one second

A wesome athletes, they are the fastest land-living creatures alive

H umans can help the cheetahs to survive and thrive.

Jack Chambers (8)
The Elms Junior School, Long Eaton

Arctic Fox

A rks are falling apart
R ivers are flowing
C limate change is causing lands to shrink
T he seas are flooding
I ce is melting
C old winds are blowing

F reezing ice begins to melt
O ver the land your countries are flooding
X enon is poisoning animals.

Ziyu (Andy) Guo (7)
The Elms Junior School, Long Eaton

Deforestation Should Stop

I want the trees putting back up again
Because they help us breathe.
I want the trees putting back up again
Because I like to climb.
I want the trees putting back up again
Because the animals need a home.
I want the trees putting back up again
Because the world loves nature.
Please stop deforestation.

Emily Walters (6)
The Elms Junior School, Long Eaton

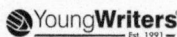

Plastic Polluting Our Underwater Planet

P oorly pufferfish panicking

L ethargic leafy sea dragons leaving

A gitated Atlantic penguins arguing

S melly jellyfish sighing

T ired turtles trembling

I rritated iridescent sharks itching

C rabby crabs crying

S ad swordfish sobbing.

Torben Brennan (6)

The Elms Junior School, Long Eaton

The World

The world loves you and me
It has lovely trees and flowers
It has given us animals and birds
And fish and insects
It has given us hills and lakes
And sun and rain
It has given us day and night
And it has given us friends and family
Now the world needs our love.

Thomas Borkowski (5)
The Elms Junior School, Long Eaton

Rainforest

Covers 6% of Planet Earth
Habitat for half our wildlife
Takes away carbon, it has such worth
It's being destroyed causing strife

Many medicines found here
Green and beautiful rainforest
Deforestation causes such fear
Save our planet, save our forest.

Hermione Wilson-Gallaher (9)
The Elms Junior School, Long Eaton

Penguins

P erfect snow is melting
E ver-increasing heat to blame
N ot enough fish to eat
G laciers falling
U nwanted pollution in the air
I ce caps collapsing
N earing extinction
S ea levels continue rising.

Eve Howat (8)
The Elms Junior School, Long Eaton

One World

Animal instinct, not animal extinct
Global warming is a warning
Be eco-friendly, recycle, reuse, refill
Plastic in our oceans can kill
Chopping down trees, deforestation
Endangering the population.

Joe Canton (8)
The Elms Junior School, Long Eaton

The Homeless Tree Frog

Haiku poetry

If there are no trees
How can I be a tree frog?
I can't live on farms

The cows will squash me
Do not chop down the trees please
You're taking my home.

Eden Faulkner (10)
The Elms Junior School, Long Eaton

199

Dolphin Poem

D eep water
O cean wide
L eaping high
P eople pleasers
H appy sounds
I ntelligent creatures
N ature's friend.

Bella Sparling (10)

The Elms Junior School, Long Eaton

Tim The Tin

My name is Tim, I am a tin
You can put me in the bin
But that would be a sin
If you recycle me
Then the world will win
Tim the tin does not go in the bin!

Leah Sood (8)

The Elms Junior School, Long Eaton

Plastic

P ollution
L ittering
A pocalypse
S ave the planet
T he planet's dying
I cebergs
C hange the world.

Rosie Faulkner (6)
The Elms Junior School, Long Eaton

YOUNG WRITERS INFORMATION

We hope you have enjoyed reading this book – and that you will continue to in the coming years.

If you're the parent or family member of an enthusiastic poet or story writer, do visit our website **www.youngwriters.co.uk/subscribe** and sign up to receive news, competitions, writing challenges and tips, activities and much, much more! There's lots to keep budding writers motivated!

If you would like to order further copies of this book, or any of our other titles, then please give us a call or order via your online account.

Young Writers
Remus House
Coltsfoot Drive
Peterborough
PE2 9BF
(01733) 890066
info@youngwriters.co.uk

Join in the conversation!
Tips, news, giveaways and much more!

 YoungWritersUK    YoungWritersCW    youngwriterscw

Scan me to watch The Big Green video!